WHAT IS SIN?

AN ATTEMPT TO ANSWER

THIS AGE-OLD QUESTION

by

Geoff Pridham

WISDOM PUBLISHING

Written 2025 by Geoff Pridham

No rights are reserved. Geoff Pridham has made this work available for anyone to copy and use however they wish.

What is Sin? by Geoff Pridham is marked with CC0 1.0 Universal. To view a copy of this license, visit
https://creativecommons.org/publicdomain/zero/1.0/

Bible quotes from *World English Bible*. Translated by Michael Paul Johnson and volunteers, eBible.org, 2020, https://ebible.org/eng-web/

Quran translation available at The Quran Academy: https://en.quranacademy.org/quran

Islamic Comprehensive Book Library "Maktaba Shamela" (in Arabic) available at: https://shamela.ws/

Cover illustration by Openclipart

ISBN: 978-0-6459378-3-1

CONTENTS

1 WHAT IS SIN? 1
2 WHAT IS SIN IN DETAIL? 25
3 CONCLUSION 93

1. WHAT IS SIN?

Sin is all around us. It is important to know what it is. That way we will be able to avoid it. But what is sin? Sin is "transgression of divine law." But what is divine law? How would we know it?

Various religious authorities tell us what God is supposed to have said and done. From their reports we are expected to know, or at least to be able to work out, what is sin in the eyes of God. We also have various old documents that are alleged to be about God or even written with the help of God. Many people believe that these documents tell us, or can help us to work out, what is sin. But there are different documents with different views and versions of God. How are we supposed to know which ones are the right ones?

Finally, in modern times not everyone believes in the old religions or buys into the truth of the old documents. How could modern people determine which is true sin and which is not if they are not even sure which version of God is the real one? How could they know if there really is a God or if that was just in the imagination of the people of the past?

With the different views presented to us by different religious authorities, old documents and modern people, how can anyone know for sure what is true sin and what is not? Is the answer so clear that no one would disagree about it? Of course not!

People today definitely do not agree on everything, including on what is "sin"… or they might call it "evil", or "wickedness", or similar terms. One thing is certain: sin sure is prevalent in the world today. It is still with us, as it has been throughout time. Why is that, after all that we have learned?

* * *

When we read the old documents some parts are easy to understand. The old ideas are clear to us. An example is the Ten Commandments. But if we look more closely at them their true meaning becomes difficult to fathom. If God wrote these then what was he really thinking or intending at the time?

Other parts of the old documents are unquestionably hard to understand. Their meaning is confusing and unclear. An example is The Garden of Eden. What was the true meaning of the fruit in the story? Why was a trickster serpent allowed into the garden?

People explore these documents and come up with different answers about their meaning. Each person says that their answer is the true meaning… the true description of what is sin, or what was in God's mind… or that these prove that there really is no God. Interesting, isn't it?

If people come up with different answers then how are we supposed to work out what the old documents really meant? We need a way to determine what God really wanted to say to us. What is that way?

Before we look for that way, let's first take a quick peek at what kinds of things the old documents say.

* * *

The old documents say things like how the earth was created, who the first people were and what they did, and God's relationship to all this.

Some old documents refer to multiple gods, or to avatars of the one supreme god. Some have very different gods from the ones we know about today. Some documents are not interested in the gods, preferring to focus on the cycles of birth and rebirth, and the attainment of nirvana. In some documents God is terrifying. In other documents he is more compassionate and merciful. In some, God calls for violence. In others, he calls for peace.

We can see that the old documents gave people different answers about the nature of the universe and our own existence. They contained different views of the world. From these world views the documents went on to tell us what would be the best way to live, or to exist. For example, the Hebrew Bible told the people of Israel that they were uniquely chosen by the one true God, Yahweh, and that they must follow his rules on how to live in order to inherit the promised land and live peacefully within it.

The old documents gave people advice, telling them what a desirable life or existence would look like. They also told people what a wrong or undesirable life would look like. The wrong choices and behaviors were explained. Where these were related to a god or gods, these wrong behaviors were labeled as "sins."

Typical sins included murder, stealing, incorrect worship, adultery, blasphemy, sexual immorality, ignoring holy days and rituals, arrogance, bearing false witness, and coveting others' property.

The opposite of sins were the desirable behaviors. These typically included faithfulness, humility before God or the gods, being just, being merciful, and being obedient to proper authority. Sometimes they included charity, chastity, patience, and simplicity in living.

In our more modern times, we have better background information about the world to work from. This puts us ahead of the people of the past in our quest to understand what is true. We know more about the world and how it operates. We also know more about ourselves and our place in the scheme of things.

Inevitably, this more accurate information changes the way we view the sins described in the old documents.

For example, when we look at the definitions of sexual immorality that are contained in the old documents we start to wonder about them. We also start to wonder about the lower position of women that is contained within the texts. We wonder about the acceptance of slavery in the documents. And we wonder about the descriptions of "inferior outside groups", such as the Philistines, the pagans, the infidels, the unbelievers, and so on. We ask ourselves questions like: "Is human slavery really okay with God?", "Is it really right to treat women as inferior to men?", "Should we really oppose people who have different views to our own?"

WHAT IS SIN?

In our modern times, we know more about the various different religions that exist in the world. This contrasts with the people of the past, who usually were only well-informed about the religion followed in their own area. With our greater knowledge we inevitably cross-compare the views of the different religions. We ask questions about which ones are truly valid and what each one implies about the best way to live.

With all this modern knowledge, how could we know which religious views are the true reflection of the real God? How could we tell which activities are sins, and which are not, in the eyes of the God who really exists?

Some of us turn away from the old answers and look only to our modern understanding to work out what might be sin and what might not be. Such people say that there is not and never was a God, or that only the God revealed to us by our modern ideas could be the real one. But how can they be sure that our modern views are more revealing of the truth than the old ones?

Others among us stay with one of the older religions. Sometimes these people resist or even denounce any modern updates to the religion of their choice.

Who is right? Is it the person who follows one of the old religions, or is it the person who only follows modern ways? If one of the old religions is the best description of truth, which one is it? Even if we do choose one of the old religions, should we believe everything that is in it, or should we only believe part of what we read? If the modern views are the only right ones, why didn't the people of the past come up with similar views? But some parts of the old documents seem to match what we think is right today! Do they really match or is that just an illusion? Maybe we could use our modern understanding to pick and choose the parts of the old documents that we think are correct. But how could we be sure that we were getting this right?

The fact is people do choose their views today. Some choose to believe the views in a particular old document, others choose to be more open-minded about it, and others choose to reject all of the old documents. People choose, but they choose differently.

Yet, we are forced to admit, not everyone can be right. There has to be a particular answer which is correct. Consider slavery: is it good? According to some old documents it is perfectly okay. Now, that can't be right. But if we choose to believe certain old documents then we will be forced to accept and implement slavery. As modern people we are left with no choice but to reject at least part of the old documents' recommendations. But when we do that we may be rejecting what God decreed. According to the old documents, God made the rules regarding slavery. If we reject slavery then are we rejecting God? Or do the old documents reflect more on the nature of the old societies that wrote them? Was God trying to improve the old societies by putting regulations in place? Or do these rules match only what the earlier people thought, having nothing to do with the true wishes of God? Immediately we can see that interpreting the past can be difficult. What was God really thinking and intending in those times?

It's as if we had different versions of God being presented to us because of the old societies that he was involved in regulating. If this is correct then how could we know which "God" was the real one and what his real intentions were? How could we know what he wanted to achieve with his actions and statements at the time? If we make a big effort and try hard to interpret what a reasonable, great and good God would have meant, can we come up with a truer picture of who he really is? Maybe he did not like slavery but could not see a workable way around it, so he came up with better, fairer regulations for carrying out slavery. He also tried to improve people's attitudes so that they would act in a kindlier manner towards each other, including towards their slaves. Maybe he wanted the human race to realize the error of its ways slowly, gradually, in its own time. This is why he did not come straight out with what he meant in full. Maybe he knew what the future would hold and he was helping us to get there in a better, milder way… or maybe he knew how to guide us to a better outcome.

How can we find an answer to all these possibilities? Maybe we could ask what God would really stand for. If we could determine that then maybe the differences between the old views and our modern ones could also be understood. It's a big question. But even if we cannot guarantee that we would be able to work out a reliable, fully-detailed answer, it is a question well worth asking. It's a question that will advance us on the road to understanding, even if we find that we can't complete the journey.

What would God really stand for? He (or she or it) would stand for what is good and right. That is obvious. We know that. And we would also like to stand for what is good and right. Of course we would! We only disagree on what good and right exactly are. But we certainly want to carry them out. When we see people wanting to do something that is obviously wrong we are dismayed by their choice. But in those people's minds the wrong thing seems right: either because they are insane, or because they think that the wrong thing is actually the right thing to do! An example is the actions of religious terrorists. They think that their terrorist acts are what God really wants them to do. We know that they are wrong, but they can't see it. The terrorists show us how important it is to understand what God really means by good and right!

People have tried to understand God's thoughts by studying the old documents, but this has resulted in many differences of opinion. When we compare the different documents we easily see that they would lead to different conclusions about what was in God's mind. We can also see why different people draw different conclusions when looking at the same document. It is not easy to work out what God was really thinking at those times.

Apart from that, there is pressure on all of us to comply with the views currently prevailing in our own area. Social pressure pushes us to agree with what is currently seen as sin and what is not. It is difficult to not comply. The person who rebels could be punished. They, at the very least, may find themselves ostracized by others.

In some areas there is dissent and disagreement. We can find ourselves being forced to agree with one group or the other. We are pushed to take a side on what is sin and what is not. But when we take a side we find ourselves in conflict with the other people, having to argue and disagree with them. It is unpleasant.

The disagreements between different groups and different areas of the earth can lead to conflict, even to full-scale conflict. This shows that working out what is really sin and what is not is absolutely essential for bringing peace to the world. Without this, conflict is inevitable.

An alternative way to bring peace to the world would seem to be for all of us to be tolerant of different viewpoints. That way, even if we couldn't agree on what was sin and what was not, we could still live peacefully with each other. But will that work all the time? Can you really be tolerant of a different view of what is sin and what is not, especially as the other person's view can be in direct conflict with your own? How can you peacefully tolerate the other person's sinful actions, in your eyes? Wouldn't you want to oppose them? Even if you wish to tolerate different viewpoints you cannot allow every evil action to be carried out… that is, evil in your eyes. You are caught by the reality of your own point of view.

Let's briefly look at some examples.

In some beliefs it is sinful for women to dress provocatively, or even attractively. Yet other belief systems have no problem with this. The result will be for the people following the first set of beliefs to experience stress when they see women dressed provocatively or even attractively. In a society that accepts multiple beliefs, the first set of believers will always be stressed. At the same time, the people who follow alternative beliefs may feel stress when they see the discrete dress of the women who follow the first set of beliefs. They may feel that those women are being unfairly restricted and even oppressed by the first set of beliefs.

One set of believers sees the provocative and attractive as sin and the other set sees modesty and discretion as a kind of sin.

Another example is terrorist murderers. These believers do not see their murdering as sin, they see it as carrying out the true wishes of their God. At the same time, the rest of us see their behavior as actual murder, which is a well-known sin covered in the Ten Commandments. Here the different beliefs have clashed irrevocably. Which one did God really want? Which one does he consider a sin?

A more minor example is the drinking of alcohol. In some beliefs it is considered sinful to drink alcohol. But in other beliefs, drinking alcohol in moderation is actually encouraged: "for your health's sake." Which one is the true sin in the eyes of God? What does he really want us to do?

Throughout history, we as individuals have had to figure out the truth for ourselves. In the past, we often had to defer to the prevailing views around us because there was so much pressure to conform. It was easier to agree and get on with the other people. It helped us to avoid trouble for ourselves. It is understandable that we did this, but even if we had been more courageous and had decided to step out on our own, how could we have been sure that we would have been able to get to the right answer? It was a struggle, because there was conflicting and confusing information available, and a lot was not known. Today, the situation has become even more difficult, as we are now often surrounded by people with different conflicting views. Even within one belief system there is disagreement over the meaning of the words in its old documents. How could we be sure that the conclusions we were forming for ourselves were really right?

In the past, the problem was compounded when the valiant truth-seeking individual could not ask the advice of anyone around them for fear of antagonizing them. If the spiritual authorities would not accept or allow any debate, and your family, friends and social contacts might unite against you, how much harder would it be to think for yourself? Some societies are still like this today. From the outside we can see how much trouble this causes for anyone who would dare to seek the truth for themselves within that oppressive society.

But would the true God accept that we did not try to find out what he really meant only because it was socially too hard for us? Couldn't that be a kind of sin too? Wouldn't he want us to seek out his true will, not ignore it just because our local religious authorities claimed this right was only for themselves? Maybe he wouldn't want us to endanger ourselves unnecessarily, so he may be happy for us to keep our discoveries to ourselves if our society was not ready to hear them. But wouldn't he want us to try to find them?

Finding the truth may not be easy, but it has to be done. If only someone could work it out and explain it properly so that everyone could understand it! Someone, or some people, must take into account all of the old documents, and also the modern knowledge about people and the world, and work out the real answers about "God." They must make the truth about God, or whatever truly represents the idea of God today, known, so that we all can see what "God" would really want us to do.

This individual, or this group of people, has to get the answer right. They have to explain it so well that everyone who hears it can finally see, and not have any doubt about, what is truly sin and what is not.

When we all finally understand what is truly sin and what is not then the world will become a better place. This is not because the world will become a perfect place, but because fewer people will carry out sinful actions based on the misunderstanding that they are not sinful, or that they are even desirable in the eyes of God. Sensible, reasonable people will no longer have to wonder why other sensible people think and do things that don't seem reasonable to them. They will know that people like themselves may have previously had mistaken beliefs, but now they can all agree. A minority may still continue to choose to sin on purpose, as such people have always done throughout history. We know that we can't stop them just by proving what is proper and right before God, because such people do not care about that! But the rest of us will agree, or at least most of us will, that this sin-choosing minority is wrong. And since what they are doing is wrong, we the majority can act together to do something about this minority's evil behavior. We will be able to act cohesively, for the first time in history, because we are so clear on what is right and what is wrong. Together, we will be able to achieve better outcomes for us all. This will be a lot less tiring than the current situation where we continually disagree and fight over what is right and what is not, as is commonplace in public life today!

* * *

Before we look at sin in more detail, let's take a moment to consider where sin comes from.

Why do we sin? With our modern knowledge, we now know that this is nature at work.

We human beings came about via evolution. Our nature is that of an evolved animal. We may be "highly evolved", but we still carry with us our ancient inheritance. Consequently, if we look at other animals we can see behaviors that are like our "sinful" ones. For example, some animals kill and eat members of other species – their "prey." We human beings also kill and eat members of other species. Some people consider that "inhumane." In other words, these people consider it a kind of sin. If it is a sin, it is still something that came from nature.

Another example is competitiveness for resources. In nature, some animals compete with each other for territory or for dominance within their group. Some animals are loners. These often have territories that they defend in some way. Other animals are more social and live in groups. Often there are dominance hierarchies within these groups. There can be one individual or a small group at the top of the hierarchy. We human beings are also social animals. We also tend to form social hierarchies with an individual or a few people at the very top. It may seem like a sin to fight to get into power, but this is something that also comes from nature. In a similar vein, it may seem like a sin for us to form groups that seek to control certain territories that we defend from outsiders in some way, but this, again, comes from nature.

Another example is favoritism. Animals have their favorites. They may prefer their own offspring over those of others in their species. In some species they may prefer one parenting partner over all the other available members of their species. In other species they may be more free and easy about who is their parenting partner. Social species may prefer the members of their own group over those of other groups of the same species. When we human beings show favoritism towards our own children, our partners, and our social group, we are doing something that comes from nature. Yet this may be a sin. Consider which creature is the most favorite of all: it is the single animal itself! When we act selfishly and favor ourselves over other people then this potential sin is something that also came from nature. When we do this we are acting very like our animal ancestors.

The last example to look at is our desires and dislikes. This covers a lot of ground in one go, but it will save us time if we look at all of these as one group. In nature, animals desire the things that are helpful for their own lives and they dislike the things that are harmful to them. They seek out the things that they desire, such as food, water, shelter, mates, and so on. They keep away from the things that they dislike, such as predators, dangers, poisonous animals and plants, strange unknown creatures, and so on. They avoid, flee or fight, as necessary. The same applies to us. We seek out our desires and avoid or attempt to destroy the things we dislike. We act on our similar animal nature. The result may lead to sin or it may have nothing to do with sin. It depends on the case and exactly how we try to carry out our wishes. But the origin of our actions is in nature.

* * *

We now know that nature may drive us to sin in some cases, but we still need to understand which actions really are sins and which are not. We still need to choose what we do, no matter what nature is telling us.

Our understanding of God throughout history is that he has sometimes asked us to do different things than what our nature is telling us. He set higher standards than those of evolution alone.

We know that the human race has always struggled between acting according to its animal nature and acting according to its understanding of what was right and good.

WHAT IS SIN?

There is nothing new here. Some of us seem to find it easier to override our simple animal nature when needed, while others, for some reason, seem to find it much harder! In any case, we need to find out what we should be overriding our animal nature to do. What, truly, is the right thing?

GEOFF PRIDHAM

2. WHAT IS SIN IN DETAIL?

To find out what is truly sin and what is not, we will go through some of the ideas of sin from the past and carefully examine them. We will extract the meaning of the sins found in the old documents, add our modern understanding, and then try to draw reasonable conclusions. We will concentrate on the three sets of monotheistic documents, as these speak directly about the will of the one true God: the Hebrew Bible (Tanakh), the Christian New Testament, and the Muslim Quran.

Let's start with the Ten Commandments.

An easy commandment to begin with is number six: "Do not murder." [Exodus (Shemot) 20:13; Deuteronomy (Devarim) 5:17]

This commandment seems obvious. All societies agree that you should not murder. But, then, certain murders are often allowed, such as during wars, court-ordered executions, and even genocide authorized by God. This may surprise you: God sometimes commanded genocide in the old documents. For example, in the Hebrew Bible, God, (whose name was "Yahweh"), ordered the people of Israel to kill all the people of Amalek, including the men, women, infants, nursing babies, and also their oxen, sheep, camels and donkeys. [Deuteronomy 25:17–19; 1 Samuel (Sefer Shmuel) 15:1–3] God applied a similar genocidal approach to the Midianites, sparing only the virgin women and girls, which the Israelites were allowed to "take for themselves." [Numbers (Bemidbar) 31:1–18] There are more examples. [Deuteronomy 7:1–2, 20:16–18; Joshua (Yehoshua) 6:1–27] God also made laws that said that witches, homosexuals and adulterers should all be killed. [Exodus 22:18; Leviticus (Wayiqra) 20:13, 20:10, 20:27] In the Muslim Quran, God ordered the killing of certain polytheists who had broken agreements with the Muslims, though he did allow them to live if they repented, performed prayers and paid the alms-tax. [Quran 9:5] So, when God said "Do not murder", he meant that this applied except when the murder was authorized by him. We must then ask ourselves: "In which cases would God authorize murder and why?"

In the old documents we find that God authorized the murder of people who did evil. This could even include their children and babies. In the Christian New Testament, we find Jesus stopping the execution of a woman by asking for the first stone to be cast by "He who is without sin." He then asked the woman to go and stop sinning. [John 8:3-11] This suggests that God can be merciful, allowing a person who has done evil to survive and repent so that they can be saved. In the Quran there are many examples of God being merciful to those who sincerely repented. The Quran begins every sura (chapter) except one with: "In the name of Allah, the Most Gracious, the Most Merciful." This shows that mercy is a fundamental part of God's nature.

The victimless crime of homosexual acts was punishable by death in the old documents. What was God's reasoning? In the Hebrew Bible, he said it was because "that is detestable" and "both of them have committed an abomination." [Leviticus 18:22, 20:13] We have to consider why he described these acts as detestable and an abomination. Together, these terms relate to abhorrence, which means disgust, repugnance and loathsomeness. God said that homosexual acts deserved death because they were disgusting, which was to such a high level that murder was required. In this case mercy could not apply. We can compare this with stealing, which was not punishable by death in the old documents. Stealing was a sin, but it may not have been a disgusting one. A detestable and abhorrent sin was for the people of Israel to worship and serve foreign Gods instead of only Yahweh. This was also punishable by death, which was to be arranged by God. [Jeremiah (Yirmeyahu) 19:3-13, 44:2-6] Creating and worshipping false idols was similarly detestable. The idols were seen as abominations by God. Worshipping them was to be punished by a death sent by God. [Ezekiel (Yekhezqel) 16:17-40] Another abomination to God was using false weights and measures. The penalty was ambiguous, but may have included the possibility of death sent by God. [Deuteronomy 25:13-16]

Other sins that were abhorrent and punishable by death included child sacrifice, marrying both a woman and her mother, sex with animals, using spirits, divination, fortune telling and sorcery. [Leviticus 20:2-5, 14-15, 27; Deuteronomy 9-12]

Why was using spirits abhorrent? The reason given in the old documents is that this leads to a turning away from God. Only God should be worshipped. Divination, fortune telling and sorcery have similar issues. Turning away from God requires the death sentence in certain cases, but in others it is God himself who will carry out the sentence. What are we to make of all this?

We have some different possible answers: (1) That God didn't say these things;

(2) That God said something different and it was changed; (3) That God could not have said these things because they are immoral; (4) That people made up these things for political purposes or because they were deluded; (5) That God really did say these things and his sayings are ethically correct. How can we know which answer is the right one? The most effective solution is for us to choose the answer that is ethically correct. Why is that? Because it is almost impossible to be certain about what happened so long ago, but if an answer is not ethical then it could not have come from the true, good God. In that case it must have come from someone other than God, such as from politically-minded people or people who were deluded in some way. Or it may even have come from a false god or evil spirit, for all we know. But an ethically correct answer may have come from the true God. If it didn't, if it really only came from people, then it will at least be okay to follow!

Which answer is ethically correct? In our modern times, we agree that murder should not be allowed. We also agree that it is acceptable to kill other people in certain circumstances, such as during wars, but only where the killing was of combatants and no alternative was available for capturing or stopping them. We do not agree to the killing of those who commit victimless acts, such as homosexual acts. We do not agree to the killing of those who worship other Gods, who consult spirits, who practice divination, fortune telling or sorcery. We are tolerant of different views and beliefs. We are absolutely opposed to the killing of children, even if they are the offspring of "evil people." Where does this place us regarding the old documents' portrayal of God's will? We are forced to disagree with it.

Since the troubling sayings are ethically incorrect, it follows that they could not have been said by the true God. If an old document contains sayings that are attributed to God, but these could not have come from the true God, then those parts of the old document cannot be trusted. Even if the majority of the old document appears to fit in with our modern ideas of what is ethical, we cannot trust those smaller unethical parts. We have to go back to our ideas about what is ethical so that we can work out what the true God would have said and done in those cases.

If a person says that the parts of an old document that contain obviously unethical ideas are the true depiction of God then that person is supporting evil. They are acting in a similar way to "sinners." When someone supports characterizations of God that show him as unethical, it is reminiscent of sin. God would not want this. The true God is a good God and does not want evil to be done. We know this would be the case if God really exists.

If God never really existed then we will still want to do what is good and right. We will not want to sin, because we are good people. But if he, she or it really does exist then we would still want to find out what that true, good God genuinely wants from us.

When we search for what is ethically correct we may make mistakes. We may find that our best thought-through decisions are wrong. In those cases we will need to backtrack and change our decisions. We will need to correct our errors. Sometimes we may find that the sayings in the old documents are better than what we have worked out for ourselves. That can happen, because we don't know everything and we are not perfect. But that does not mean that we should adopt the sayings in the old documents without trying to assess them first. Our horror at the commands in the old documents to commit genocide shows us that the ethics must be checked before we accept what we are being told. We need to be careful about what we choose to follow because it may lead us away from the true good and into actual sin.

What is actual good, then? It is doing what benefits other people. And it is also *not* doing what harms them. Then what is sin? It is the intention to cause harm to other people. And it is also deliberately avoiding doing what benefits them. What is not sin is the intention to benefit other people. These are the basic guidelines we can apply to our understanding of the intentions of the true, good God. If he, she or it really exists then this is what the true God would want from us.

How do these guidelines apply to murder? Murder is the intention to harm other people and so it is a sin to commit it. Yet there may be cases where the other person is trying to carry out evil actions. In some of these cases we may be forced to kill or injure the other person in order to prevent them from causing further harm. This would not be a sin because it was done to protect and help others and there was no other option. If we have captured a murderer and they cannot cause any further harm then it would be a sin to kill them at this point. This is because we have the power to prevent them from causing harm without killing them. If we did not have that power then executing them may be the only option, as can happen during combat in times of war. These are the kind of answers we get when we apply our ethical guidelines to understanding the sin of murder. This is what the true God would really want... to the best of our understanding today.

* * *

Before we continue with our examination of the Ten Commandments we are forced to take a break so we can check if our idea of good is really right. We have said that good is doing what benefits other people, and not doing what harms them, but how do we know if that applies to everyone equally or if it applies only to the right kind of people? We have to ask this question because the people of ancient times clearly thought that good applied only to particular groups of people. They also thought that good applied more to certain people inside their own communities, such as the leaders and priests, and less to others, such as the women and slaves... generally speaking. We have to answer that. Is good for everyone, and should it be applied equally?

In the old documents we have seen that genocide was commanded by God in certain cases. This implies that the people who were to be exterminated, including their children and babies, did not deserve to live. As we saw earlier, even in the peace-orientated religion of Islam there was a case in the Quran where the merciless killing of enemies was commanded. (Except if they repented, performed prayers and paid the alms-tax.) Some Islamic interpreters have thought that this passage meant that murdering unbelievers was encouraged by God. The majority of Islamic thinkers have not agreed with that, but the fact that some people could interpret the passage this way shows that people can believe that good is not equal for everyone, including in the eyes of God. If we turn our attention to the Christian New Testament we find Jesus, the Son of God, saying that the goats will be separated from the sheep, and that the weeds will be separated from the wheat and thrown into the fire. [Matthew 25:31-46; 13:24-30] Since Jesus represents the thinking of God, it follows that God is making distinctions between types of people. Some will be more deserving of the good and some will not be. This will be decided at some point during or after their lives on Earth. If God can make this distinction then why can't we?

Why can't we? The reason is that we are far from perfect. We are not all-wise and all-knowing. Our judgments are influenced by our animal ancestry, where we naturally hate our enemies and want to take revenge on those who have hurt us. That comes from evolution. But if we were to judge perfectly, the way God is believed to do, then we would easily ignore our human feelings and judge only via the totality of the facts involved. But we are not like that. We cannot easily ignore our human emotions and we never have all the facts of the case for another human being. If we cannot judge an individual person fully then how much less can we get the judgments of whole groups of people right! Still, our human nature will do this anyway: it will judge all over the place. It is interesting that in the old documents, Jesus said "Do not judge…", preferring for us to "Love your neighbor as yourself." [Matthew 7:1-5, 19:19, 22:39] It seems that he was well aware of the limitations of our human minds.

The people of ancient history had preferences. First, they preferred the people of their own area. Second, they preferred their higher-status people. Third, they preferred those who obeyed their social rules. All these things came from their human minds. These preferences naturally arose from their human emotions. We have to be careful not to fall into the same trap. We must not "naturally" prefer the people of our own area, nor those with higher status, nor those who obey our current social rules. We have to form better, fairer judgments than these. This is why our definition of good has to cover *all* people.

Finally, we have to ask about God's judgments. If God can judge perfectly then shouldn't we follow his instructions on whom to kill? If he said that all of the people of Amalek were to be killed then doesn't that show that they were completely evil? That makes sense, except for one little question: how do we know that God really said that? In the case of Amalek, the prophet Samuel told King Saul what God, Yahweh of Hosts, had said. Samuel passed on God's instructions to kill all the people of Amalek, including the children and babies. At least, the old document says this. [1 Samuel 15:1-3] How can we know, to a level that we can be sure enough about, that this really happened and that God really said this through his prophet Samuel? We have to be very confident about this, because this is about genocide. This is about killing nursing babies. We cannot afford to get this wrong!

Consider how many times we have been asked to believe vicious instructions because they were reported to be from God. How many of these came from the mouths of men, and how many came to us directly from the mouth of God? Almost all have come from the mouths of men. Those that were reported to have come from God have been relayed to us by people. We mostly know about these through the old documents, though some have been reported after those ancient times. We know that people can lie or be deluded. How can we be sure that they are relaying the actual truth to us about God's sayings? Is there some way to know, beyond reasonable doubt?

The most effective solution has to be the same as we said before: choose the answer that is ethically correct. If the words of God that people are relaying to us match what is ethically correct then they may really reflect God's will. But if they seem to stray from what is ethically correct then they have almost certainly been modified in some way:

either by mistake or misunderstanding, or through delusion, or, worst of all, through deceit. As we said before, they may even have been told to the person by some kind of evil spirit! Ethics will show us the way. Ethics will tell us what is most likely to be really happening.

Knowing that we have our misleading human emotional prejudices and preferences, that we cannot be sure that someone relaying the words of God is telling the truth or getting it right, and that when God appears to have told us to commit major evils this seems to contradict the idea of him being a good God, then we have to be very careful before we carry out major crimes in God's name. The safer course is to find out what a true, good God would really think. If the relayed message does not match that then something must be seriously wrong.

* * *

Before we return to the commandments, let's strongly challenge our idea that good should apply to all people. We have to do this because many people, including some in religious authority, have given opposing answers to this question. For example, some religious authorities have said that certain individuals are definitely less deserving of good treatment than others, and that this can even apply to whole groups of people. These authorities have sometimes referred to the old documents' troubling areas as support for their views. What are we to make of this? What can we say in response? Do the old texts really prove that some individuals are less deserving of good treatment, and that this can also apply to whole groups of people?

Even if we ignore the troubling parts in the old documents, the fact is that many people believe, (or at least they act as if they believe), that some people are less deserving of good treatment than others. This is happening even in our more enlightened times. How could we contradict that? What would be our argument?

Imagine that we had God's understanding: what would our judgment of people be like then? It would be perfect. We would be able to say, with absolute conviction, who deserved what and when. Compare that with what God actually does. Does he openly remove people from earth all the time, throwing them into "the fires of hell?" If he is doing this, he is not making it obvious. Does he save all the saints (the true followers) from harm? That is not what we have seen in history. In fact, the saints often had to suffer for their faith. Whatever that means requires interpretation. God is not fully revealing his hand. If God can judge perfectly, why doesn't he just go ahead and do that? Why does he let evil people commit their horrific crimes? Why does he let good people suffer and even sometimes die at the hands of the wicked? There must be a reason.

The most obvious reason, believed by a number of people today, is that there is no God. That would explain the "hiding of his hand." But could there be a different reason: one that matches his existence and what we see happening in the world? It could be that he is holding off his judgment… delaying it. Why would he be doing that? It could be that he is giving us chances, even to the very wicked among us. But why would God need to give chances to horrible people when he already knows what they are and what they are going to be? The most obvious answer is that he doesn't know what they are going to be, at least not for sure. Since he doesn't know all the outcomes, he is waiting to see what will happen. Then, when the moment is right, he will be able to act. Isn't this an attitude that we should want to emulate?

For those who believe that there is no God, or that God is not similar to what we have just described, the judgment of others is still an open issue. However, the same question applies: can those people really know the ultimate outcome for all other people? For example, if someone is clearly wicked today, can we be sure that this person will always be wicked? If we can't, what should we do in regard to judging that person?

When we said that our definition of good has to cover *all* people, we meant that even the blatantly wicked should be covered. "Good" should apply to them. In other words, we should want to benefit them and not to harm them too, even knowing that what they are doing, and what they want to do, is wrong. We don't mean this in a crazy way. We mean that these wicked people should be covered by our good wishes, but not that they should be allowed to continue harming others. On our planet, in our human world, we can use what power we have to act directly on these wicked people. We can do our best to stop them from committing their crimes… but our intentions towards them will always be good. We will always be hoping for their "salvation", their turning to good, while remaining well aware that most of the time they will not change their ways, and, of course, we will sensibly continue our attempts to stop them from carrying out their evil intentions on us and the world!

***

The next commandment we will look at is number eight: "Do not steal." [Exodus 20:15; Deuteronomy 5:19]

This commandment is easy to understand. Yet in the old documents we find that it was okay to steal from certain groups of people. We have already seen that Yahweh authorized the Israelites to "take for themselves" the virgin women and girls of the Midianites, rather than execute them. In other cases, Yahweh gave the land of other nations to the Israelites on the basis that he did not like the behavior of these nations and preferred that of the Israelites. [Deuteronomy 7:1, 12:29, 19:1, 20:13-14; Numbers 33:53] The reasoning seems to have been that the nations that worshipped evil, false gods and did not behave ethically did not deserve to stay in the land. They could surrender to the Israelites and leave, or they could be completely destroyed. Nothing that related to their evil, false gods was to be retained, it was all to be destroyed. But the land was to be given to the people chosen by Yahweh, as they were to become an example of good behavior and proper worship for the world.

It is interesting that Yahweh thought that conquered women could be treated like possessions. When he allowed the Israelites to "take for themselves" the virgin women and girls of the Midianites he implied that they could be possessed. However, the general ancient views on slavery meant that all people could become possessions, regardless of their gender. In the case of Israel, Yahweh set a limit on how long an Israelite person could serve another without freedom. The limit was six years, unless the person asked to stay in service after that time. [Deuteronomy 15:12-18]

A more recent idea (from 1840) regarding stealing is the famous saying of Pierre-Joseph Proudhon (which interested Karl Marx): "Property is theft." By this he meant that it was a form of robbery to exploit other people's labor without making any effort of your own, simply because you "owned" the means for production, such as owning the land that others must farm. If a person controls the means for the production of wealth then are they, in effect, "stealing" it from others? We could expand this further: if a person controls a situation in such a way that they, or they and their friends, profit more than others, is that like stealing? If it is then it follows that all powerful people who do not act fairly are, in effect, stealing from the less powerful (or whomever they unfairly harm). Since we all have some form of power, for example, being citizens of a richer country, we can expand the statement to say that whoever uses their power unfairly, (even if this is a small power), is using that power to effectively steal from their victims (even if this is a small theft). How does the commandment look now!

Our definition of stealing now covers all forms of theft. Even if we are born in a richer, more powerful country we may unwittingly be stealing from the poorer, less powerful places on Earth! Even if we use what little power we have in our own lives in a way that is not completely fair, we may be committing a form of stealing... which is a sin, against the eighth commandment. We don't want to go too far with this, it could not be a major sin to use a little power slightly unfairly, but doing so is against the *spirit* of the commandment. If we genuinely want to follow God's will then we must make an effort to not use our power unfairly, whatever that power may be.

Some thieves justify their actions by saying that they are "taking back" what should have been rightly theirs in the first place.

We can see why this argument could make some sort of sense, because the unfair use of power does take away from those in a less powerful position. On the other hand, we cannot agree with the solution of actually stealing, no matter what reason is behind it. This solution directly contradicts the eighth commandment. It cannot be right.

Better solutions to the unfairness of "property" are to apply reasonable taxes to the rich, provide welfare to those in need – including those in other nations, and encourage charitable donations and actions. For the unfair application of power, better solutions include implementing a robust democracy, outlawing slavery, making legal processes available to all, and making arrogant behavior in power socially unacceptable.

We should not steal, we should not cheat, we should not abuse our power. We should be benevolent and kind. That is what a good God would want from us.

* * *

The next commandments to examine are numbers one and two, summarized as: "Do not have any false gods before me."

In detail these are:

"1. You shall have no other gods before me."

"2. You shall not make a carved image for yourself – any likeness of what is in heaven above, or what is in the earth beneath, or that is in the water under the earth. You shall not bow yourself down to them, nor serve them, for I, Yahweh your God, am a jealous God, visiting the iniquity of the fathers on the children and on the third and on the fourth generation of those who hate me and showing loving kindness to thousands of those who love me and keep my commandments." [Deuteronomy 5:7-10]

We see that Yahweh is jealous of the worship of any other gods, whether they be real or false. We also have an ambiguous statement about who will be punished if someone goes against him: "visiting the iniquity" is very vague – does it mean punishment or does it mean that he keeps an eye on the succeeding generations of the evildoer in case they also do evil? Perhaps he was just warning people that their evils could affect their descendants. It is not clear. There are various translations of the old document. Some say that "visiting the iniquity" is "punishing", but others do not say this. What are we to think? If God is saying that the children and the next two generations are all to be punished then he would not be acting ethically. Ethical behavior may allow punishing those who did something wrong, but not their innocent offspring. Obviously, if their offspring were also guilty of sinful behavior then they would be deserving of punishment, but only if that was the case. Since the true God is a good God it follows that "visiting the iniquity" must be a warning to the parents to behave properly, lest they cause any problems for their descendants.

If we look ahead in the Hebrew Bible to Ezekiel (Yekhezqel), chapter 18, we find Yahweh telling the prophet Ezekiel that a man shall not be punished if he does the right things, no matter what his son does. Also, a son who does the right thing will not be punished, no matter what his father has done. In verse 20 we read: "The son shall not bear the iniquity of the father, neither shall the father bear the iniquity of the son. The righteousness of the righteous shall be on him, and the wickedness of the wicked shall be on him." From this we can see that our idea was correct that God was warning the parents to behave properly in order to prevent problems for their descendants. He was not condemning those who were innocent. This matches our version of a good God who is ethical and fair.

Why would a good God be jealous of the worship of false or other gods? If those other gods were made up by people, why would he be jealous? If the other gods were not gods but were instead evil spirits masquerading as gods, why would a good God be jealous of them? It must be that this jealousy in the commandments was a warning to people that following other gods would only bring them trouble. Following the true good God would bring them benefits. The ideas of love and hate towards God may have been simple ways to communicate with ancient people. The true God would not be a simple-minded emotional being: he (or she or it) would be an advanced, deep-thinking, ethical one. But, he may have found it easier to get his good points across to the primitive, uneducated people of the past by using the simple, emotional terms that they would easily understand. This idea matches our version of what a true good God would be like, while not contradicting the text in the old documents.

There is a danger in the idea that people are condemned simply because they do not love God, or even "hate" him. Believers can take this to mean that some people are to be condemned because they have different beliefs. What if there are multiple versions of God in the world? Then the believers of one version may think that the followers of other versions are worshipping false gods and so deserve to be punished. The "iniquities" should be visited on them. Yet the true good God would never have meant this. The good God would have wanted people to follow what was true and right, and to do good to others. The commandment to worship only the true God was meant to guide people towards what was right and good. It was not meant to give people the authority to condemn others. This is especially true if those others were also doing what was good and right. The commandment is not about the jealousy of God, it is about the need to do what is right. It was simply expressed in a way that the people of ancient times could follow. We might say that it was an attempt to lead them out of their ignorance and barbarism towards knowledge and advanced ethical behavior!

* * *

The next commandment to examine is number seven: "You shall not commit adultery." [Exodus 20:14; Deuteronomy 5:18]

Adultery was punishable by death. [Leviticus 20:10] Why did God assign such a harsh punishment to this sin? In modern times we often see adultery as a kind of "non-crime." It may be annoying and disrespectful to the affected partner, but it is not punishable by death or even by time in prison. Why have we moved from seeing this as an extremely unacceptable sin towards it being a very minor one? What would a good God say about our change of attitude?

Adultery is a kind of stealing from your partner. In this sense it causes harm to the other person. It is a breach of trust, a breaking of an agreement. It is obvious that breaking an agreement would not normally warrant death. The solution would be to allow the victim to be freed from the relationship, if they wish. Any financial impact on the victim should be corrected, as much as possible. Other people should be cautious about trusting the sinner in future as they have shown that they are capable of breaking agreements. Why, then, is the death of the sinner required in the old documents? The reason found in the text is not clear: adultery is simply seen as a major crime. It is doing something "impure." The nearest we can get to finding an answer is when Yahweh describes the people of Israel as being adulterous towards him. Yahweh complains that his people worship false gods, the gods of other lands. This is adultery, because Israel is supposed to only worship him. This is a serious offense, warranting great punishments for the Israelites if they will not repent and turn from their evil ways. Perhaps adultery against marriage partners was seen as a major offense because it reflected all kinds of promise breaking, including the major breach of faith against Yahweh. This may be the reasoning behind killing the adulterers – that this kind of behavior should be avoided at all costs by Israel, so that all faithful commitments would be honored without question. If that is correct then we have to ask: "Is this what a good God would do?"

Our ethical answer would have to be "No." A good God would not have people killed just so that they got into the habit of obeying all his rules, following him without question. That is too extreme. So what are we to think of this old text? It could not be a rule which was made murderous just to ensure that the Israelites got into the habit of obeying God. It must be taken at face value, which means that adultery was seen by God as a major sin. Before we try to judge the God of the Hebrew Bible, let's take another look at the other sins that warranted death.

The sins that warranted death included homosexual acts, child sacrifice, marrying both a woman and her mother, sex with animals, using spirits, divination, fortune telling and sorcery. We examined these earlier and concluded that where this ruling was not ethical it could not have come from the true good God. It must have come from either the feelings of the ancient people or the political needs of their societies. We said that the parts of the old documents that attribute unethical decisions to God could not be trusted. These would need to be examined carefully and compared with our modern understanding of ethics before deciding if they reflected the actual God or not.

We can see a pattern in the unethical, extremist laws that were said to have been made by God. The pattern is that the Israelites were being instructed to follow Yahweh in all aspects of their lives and not to stray in any way from that. They were not to be "adulterous" and follow foreign gods, and they were not to be "impure", instead remaining clean and "sanctified" to Yahweh. In return, Yahweh promised to look after them. If they went against these things then they would be punished. This pattern explains the political need for adultery to be punishable by death. Any sin that led to a turning away from Yahweh needed to be stopped. The fear of death should have been a strong way to prevent those sins.

Consider Yahweh himself: as an advanced ethical being, would he want people to follow him because they feared the punishments he put in place for them? Wouldn't it make more sense for him to explain why the behaviors were wrong? We can accept the view that the people of those ancient times were primitive and barbarous, but does that mean that there was no other means for making them more educated and civilized? Was the death sentence for incorrect political behavior the only way to lead them toward a better world?

Our rule for judging the old documents is that their version of God must match the best ethics that we can work out. If they fail to do this then they cannot be representing the true good God. We may make mistakes in this approach, but this is better than accepting that "God is evil." We cannot and must not carry out extreme actions without checking what we are doing first. If we accept the old documents' version of God as unquestionably and completely true then we will certainly become sinners ourselves.

The fact that the God portrayed in the old documents is clearly unethical, at least for some of the time, must tell us that he was a sinner at those times. Since the true God could not be a sinner, the only conclusion we can reasonably draw is that the texts are not completely correct. Whenever the old documents propose unethical actions and attribute them to God, those parts of the text are wrong.

* * *

The idea that parts of the old documents must be wrong is a major one. It is extremely controversial and could not be easily accepted by the authorities supporting the various religions. But, then, these same authorities dispute the validity of the old documents that are outside their own religion. Followers of Judaism believe that Christianity and Islam are not correct. Followers of Christianity do not believe that the Quran came from God. Followers of Islam believe that the Hebrew and Christian documents are not completely accurate reflections of what really happened in the past. If they can dispute the accuracy of other documents, why can't they consider the possibility of inaccuracies existing in their own documents?

The reason is obvious. If an authority was to question the validity of what was in their own religion's documents then their own authority would come into question. Why would people follow their lead if they were questioning its very basis themselves? It would be better for religious authorities to do their questioning in private, among themselves, than to let the public see it. Maybe after enough of the authority's peers had agreed to some change in interpretation then the new truth could be revealed to the followers. A united front from the top should allow changes to be implemented without too much loss of power. Such is the political thinking necessitated for religious authorities.

To be fair, authorities may indeed have doubts about some aspects of the reporting in their old documents. But they will be forced to discuss these in discreet ways rather than openly, for fear of the repercussions. They need to put forward their doubts in an acceptable manner to their colleagues, who will need to be careful about how they discuss the matter. When enough of them agree on the doubted area, the authoritative group will need to figure out a safe way to convey this to the larger group of less-informed believers. It will take care and time to safely achieve the change. This kind of thing has been done throughout the history of each religion. We can see that the views about the will of God have changed over time. The definition of what exactly is sin and what exactly should be the penalty for it has changed in history. For example, the death penalty for adultery is not carried out by today's "Israelites."

The sin of homosexual acts is punished with death in the Hebrew Bible. The reasoning was that this was "detestable" and "an abomination", as we discussed before. These words show that this was not a moral judgment but one that was based on extremely strong feelings. The judgment had minor or even no political implications for that society, consequently, it must have been one that was about the feelings of those ancient people. Not all ancient societies were opposed to homosexual acts, so we can say that revulsion for them is not mandatory for human beings. The ancient Israelites did not like them, that was the common feeling in their society, and that is why it was believed that God did not like them either. The same dislike is shown in the Christian New Testament and the Muslim Quran, though neither of these proposes that the death penalty should be carried out by people. The New Testament documents equate homosexual acts with other sins, such as murder, slave-trading, lying, perjury, ungodliness, lawlessness, insubordination, unrighteousness, wickedness, covetousness, malice, envy, strife, secret slander, backbiting, insolence, arrogance, boasting, disobedience to parents, breaking covenants, being unforgiving and unmerciful. [Romans 1:26–27; 1 Timothy 1:8–10] Why was this victimless act associated with so much evil? The statements were not quoting God but were the views of the apostle Paul. Paul was a Jew who was originally a member of the Pharisees, a religious party that carefully studied the Hebrew Bible. We can see from this that he would have viewed homosexual acts as a major sin. His statements against the people who engaged in them matched his background. We then have to ask: what did Jesus think about homosexuality?

In the New Testament documents, Jesus never refers to homosexual acts directly. He did speak against sexual immorality in general. Jesus was a Jew and was also knowledgeable about the Hebrew Bible, so his idea of sexual immorality could include homosexual acts, even if he did not spell this out in the old documents. What should we conclude?

The obvious conclusion is that Jewish people in ancient times were opposed to homosexual acts. They had strong feelings against them. Their strong feelings were not common to all societies, however. For example, the Ancient Egyptians, Greeks and Romans were not opposed. Since this "sin" has no victims, it follows that a good God could not have proposed the death sentence for it. Consequently, these parts of the old documents must reflect the feelings of the ancient people involved, rather than the will of God. We have to accept that parts of the old documents are wrong, otherwise we would sometimes be following an unethical version of God. Even if our knowledge of it is imperfect, the test of ethics can guide us when we are trying to decide which parts of the old documents to believe and which cannot be right.

* * *

The remaining commandments to examine are three, four, five, nine and ten.

Three is: "You shall not misuse the name of Yahweh your God, for Yahweh will not hold him guiltless who misuses his name." [Exodus 20:7]

This commandment is easy to understand. It would be rude and disrespectful to use the name of God wrongly, such as in swearing. No one should be treated this way, let alone the true God.

Four is: "Remember the Sabbath day, to keep it holy. You shall labor six days, and do all your work, but the seventh day is a Sabbath to Yahweh your God. You shall not do any work in it, you, nor your son, nor your daughter, your male servant, nor your female servant, nor your livestock, nor your stranger who is within your gates; for in six days Yahweh made heaven and earth, the sea, and all that is in them, and rested the seventh day; therefore Yahweh blessed the Sabbath day, and made it holy." [Exodus 20:8-11]

This commandment provided a benefit to working people. They were guaranteed a day of rest each week. God was showing us the way to provide good working conditions for people, not unfair, harmful ones. This is a lesson many companies and countries need to relearn today! Those who are happy to harm others in order to benefit themselves should not be the ones making the decisions. Our societies should take back control from such selfish people and ensure fair, safe and proper working conditions for all.

Five is: "Honor your father and your mother, that your days may be long in the land which Yahweh your God gives you." [Exodus 20:12]

What could this mean? Parents are not always honorable people. They can be sinners, seeking to cause harm to others.

Should people like that be honored? Obviously not. In the light of that, what could God have meant?

The clue is in the "land." The second part of the commandment refers to the land that Yahweh is giving to the Israelites. They will live long there if they honor their parents. This shows that the Israelites should follow the traditions handed down to them, as these came from Yahweh, who gave them the land. If they follow the good and reject the bad then they will be well off. Their "parents" are just a representation of doing what is right and avoiding what is wrong.

We, also, should do what is right and good, what benefits other people and does not harm them. If our "parents" hand us a tradition that harms others and does not benefit them then we should equally reject that tradition. Honor the good and dishonor the bad, whether it comes from tradition or not.

Nine is: "You shall not give false testimony against your neighbor." [Exodus 20:16]

This is a very obvious commandment, not needing any explanation.

Ten is: "You shall not covet your neighbor's house. You shall not covet your neighbor's wife, nor his male servant, nor his female servant, nor his ox, nor his donkey, nor anything that is your neighbor's." [Exodus 20:16]

Why does God describe coveting as a sin? The action of stealing is a sin because it harms the other person, but how can the action of desiring someone else's property harm them? Obviously, it can't. But it could lead you into stealing one day. If you avoid coveting then you will be less likely to actually harm the other person. Is this what God meant?

Another possibility is that God wanted people to follow the spirit of the law. The law was not just about doing the right thing, it was about thinking the right thing. In other words, the chosen people should become the actually good people: people who were ethical, who sought to do good to others and not to harm them. If their thoughts were about coveting then they would be about harming. But if their thoughts were not about doing bad things then they might turn into ones about doing good things. Perhaps this is what God was driving at.

In the Christian New Testament, Jesus says similar things about thinking bad thoughts. He says that if your right eye causes you to stumble, because it looks at a woman lustfully, you should pluck it out and cast it from you. It is better that one part of you should be lost than for your whole body to be cast into Gehenna (hell). [Matthew 5:29] He says a similar thing about the right hand. [Matthew 5:30] The implication is that you should not just obey the letter of the law, you should follow the spirit of the law. This matches our idea that God wants us to have good thoughts, not just commit to doing good actions. We should also avoid having bad thoughts, not just refrain from doing evil.

* * *

We have finished looking at the Ten Commandments. The next idea we can look at is the Golden Rule. In the old documents, Jesus said: "As you desire that men should do to you, likewise do to them also." [Luke

6:31] This is expanded in Matthew: "Therefore whatever you desire for men to do to you, you shall also do to them; for this is the law and the prophets." [Matthew 7:12] The expanded version shows that the Golden Rule is a summary of the Hebrew Bible ideas. A similar statement in the Hebrew Bible is: "You shall not take vengeance, nor bear any grudge against the children of your people; but you shall love your neighbor as yourself. I am Yahweh." [Leviticus 19:18] What do these statements mean?

These statements are about the basis of advanced ethics. Ethics is about doing good and not doing evil, which means providing benefits to others and not harming them. If we treat other people "as ourselves", we have opened the door to wanting to do good to them and not to harm them… at least, in theory. If we were of sound mind we would want others to benefit us and to not harm us, obviously. A sinner is acting according to their animal nature. They may place their preferences on themselves and those nearest to them. Such a person will easily treat others differently to themselves, seeking to do good only to themselves and those they value, and indifferent to doing harm to those they see as being outside this group. The Golden Rule speaks directly to them. It clearly tells them to change.

What if we are the victims of sinful people – those who blindly follow their animal nature? What should we do for them? According to the Golden Rule, we should want to benefit them, not to harm them in return. But what would benefit a person blindly acting in sin? If we don't stop their sinful actions then we will be allowing them to continue to harm others, including ourselves. Would that be the right thing for us to do? It's not just the sinful person whom we have to consider when applying the Golden Rule: other people have a place in our decision making. How can we protect others and ourselves while also benefiting the sinner... and not harming them?

Can we find an answer by studying the other sayings of Jesus in the old documents? Jesus proposed that the evils of the dominating Roman Empire should not be resisted. He said to pay the Roman taxes, not to take up the sword, love your enemies, bless those who curse you, do good to those who hate you, and pray for those who spitefully use you and persecute you. [Mark 12:17; Matthew 26:52, 5:44] Why were we to do these things? Jesus explained it was so that: "you may be sons of your Father who is in heaven. For he makes his sun to rise on the evil and the good, and sends rain on the just and the unjust." [Matthew 5:45] He concluded that "Therefore you shall be perfect, just as your Father in heaven is perfect." [Matthew 5:48] How do these statements help us to answer our question?

Jesus appears to be saying that we should follow the Golden Rule even at our own expense, including the expense of those around us. His reasoning was that God was doing exactly the same thing. His statement that God was doing the same thing could not have meant that God did not punish the wicked, as that happened many times in the Hebrew Bible documents. Nor could it mean that God didn't help the good, as that also happened many times in the old documents. What could he have really meant, then? When we read the entire speech in Matthew chapter 5, we see that Jesus was saying that the entire law should be followed down to the smallest level, including following the spirit of the law. In fact, the spirit of the law was the whole point of the law. The law reflected the perfect nature of God. If we emulated the same perfect nature then we would not need the law because we would be following it perfectly… automatically. We would generate the same actions that God would… if he were us in our shoes.

If we try to emulate the perfect nature of God then we will come closer to knowing the answer for how to treat sinful people when we and others would be their victims. What would this be like?

The perfect nature of God is not one without justice, but it is one with a lot of mercy and compassion. It is "loving your neighbor as yourself." How would we treat the sinner who is acting against us if we loved them as if they were ourselves? Imagine that we were the sinner, harming others deliberately: what would we want? At first we might think that the sinner would want to be able to continue harming others without restriction, but if we think a little further we might realize that the mind of the sinner is not at peace: it is not in the best state that is available. The mind that is in the best state is the mind that is closest to God's. In other words: the mind of the highly ethical person, the one that wants to "love its neighbor as itself." It follows that the best thing that we could do for the sinner is to help them on the road to attaining a highly ethical mind. But how could this be done… and what does it mean in practical terms?

In practical terms, we should prevent the sinner from harming other people any further… if that is possible. And we should do this in a way that does not harm the sinner, as much as that is possible. There is nothing complex in this idea, it is easy to understand. Over the centuries our law enforcement systems have been moving towards this goal. There is still some way to go, but progress has been made. The direction we need to travel in is clear.

What about changing the mind of the sinner? How do we go about doing that? In my view it is, as far as I can determine, almost impossible. This is a great shame, because the person who chooses to harm others may never know what it is like to be "the friend of all." Their gloomy, hostile world will continue to exist, inside their own mind. Still, this is the goal we should aim for. We should try to find a way to "reach" the person inside the sinner and show them that the welfare of their neighbor really should be incorporated into their thoughts. Then they would be truly free. Free from the darkness that is in their mind. If only they could be saved!

We do not need to give up all hope on "sinners" being saved because it has happened before. One example was the writer of the well-known hymn "Amazing Grace." This person, John Newton, was an English slave trader. He converted to Christianity after praying to God to save his ship from a fierce thunderstorm in 1748. He studied the Bible and in time he realized that slavery was wrong. He wrote the hymn and also a book, *Thoughts upon the African Slave Trade*, which revealed how evil this practice was. He became an Anglican priest and also a slavery abolitionist. This shows that change is possible in the minds of people who choose to harm others.

How can we help people to change? I do

not know the best answer, but one thing is certain: we must explain our point of view clearly! The reasons for us saying that the Golden Rule should apply are that: (1) It is the only way that a civilization that includes all people could run smoothly; (2) It is the only way we could all live in peace together; (3) It is the truth about our actual relationship to all other people; and (4) It gives us the best state of mind that we can experience towards the world.

The conclusion about God's wishes regarding the Golden Rule is that we should do good and not evil! In other words, we should seek to benefit others and not to harm them. This would not be sin.

* * *

The next area we can look at is drinking alcohol. In the Muslim Quran, after some earlier verses were less restrictive about it, this was finally forbidden. [Quran: 5:90] God's reasoning was that intoxicants and gambling were from Satan and were intended to defile the believer. They should be avoided if the believer was to succeed in their quest to be good. In other old documents, God did not prohibit drinking alcohol, but he did dislike drunkenness. [Isaiah 5:22, 28:1-7] Those who wanted to make a special vow of dedication to Yahweh were not to drink any wine or other fermented drink during the time of their dedication. [Numbers 6:3] Priests were not to drink wine when they were going to enter the inner court of the temple. [Ezekiel 44:21] There are examples in the old documents of drunkenness leading to problems for people, including causing them to disrespect God. [Genesis (Bereshit) 9:21-25; Deuteronomy 21:18-21] What would be our conclusion?

It is obvious that God was against drunkenness. The reason was that it could encourage people to act sinfully and to disrespect God and his laws. Alcohol or other intoxicants do not necessarily lead to "drunkenness", but the user should be careful to not allow this to happen. The safest course would be to avoid all intoxicants, but it has not been proved that it is a sin to indulge in them in moderation. However, for a Muslim it is definitely written that it is a sin: they should not touch intoxicants.

Is alcohol good for your health? There have been a few debates about this in our modern times. In the New Testament, Paul recommends to Timothy that he not just drink water but use a little wine for his stomach's sake and his frequent infirmities. [1 Timothy 5:23] This suggests that ancient people thought that a little wine may help with their health. Similar claims have been made today, but a comprehensive study published in 2018 in *The Lancet* concluded that "alcohol is a colossal global health issue and small reductions in health-related harms at low levels of alcohol intake are outweighed by the increased risk of other health-related harms, including cancer. There is strong support here for the guideline published by the Chief Medical Officer of the UK who found that there is 'no safe level of alcohol consumption'."

[DOI: https://doi.org/10.1016/S0140-6736(18)31571-X]

The view of the World Health Organization, published in *The Lancet* in January 2023, was that "no safe amount of alcohol consumption for cancers and health can be established."

[DOI: https://doi.org/10.1016/S2468-2667(22)00317-6]

Is drinking alcohol for a non-Muslim a sin? It certainly cannot be recommended for health, nor for the dangers of drunkenness. A good God would not want people to be harmed and so would not recommend the use of alcohol. He may not make it a sin to drink in moderation, but he would strongly recommend not drinking it at all, for your health's sake!

* * *

The next area is our mode of dress. In some old documents it is considered a sin for women to dress provocatively or even attractively. Is this what God meant?

In the Quran, God says that clothes are to conceal our private parts and as adornment. He then recommends that the best is "the clothing of righteousness" that is from "the signs of Allah" so that they may remember. [Quran 7:26] This applies to all believing people, both men and women. In another sura, he says that believing men should lower their gaze and guard their chastity (sometimes translated as modesty or private parts). [Quran 24:30] Believing women should also lower their gaze, guard their chastity and not display their adornment except what is apparent. They should draw their head covers over their bosoms and not display their adornment except to appropriate people, such as their husbands, fathers, fathers-in-law, sons, brothers, nephews, their women, male attendants who don't have physical desires, and children who are not aware of the private aspects of women. They should not stamp their feet to make known what they conceal of their adornment. [Quran 24:31] Another verse recommends that believing women should draw over themselves their outer garments, as "That is more suitable that they should be known and not harmed." [Quran 33:59] This outer garment was any sort that fits loosely over and around other clothes and is related to local customs and culture. There is much debate over the exact meaning of "adornment", "what is apparent" (that which can be displayed), and what was a "head cover." What would a good God have been driving at?

In the Christian New Testament, Paul says that he wants believing women to adorn themselves in decent clothing, with modesty and propriety; not just with braided hair, and gold or pearls or costly clothing; but (which becomes women professing godliness) through good works. [1 Timothy 2:9-10] But this is not stated to be God speaking. In the Hebrew Bible, being seen naked was considered shameful. God also says he dislikes Israelite women acting haughty, walking with outstretched necks and flirting eyes, walking to trip as they go, jingling ornaments on their feet. [Isaiah 3:16] In general, God prefers humility and dislikes haughtiness and proud boasting. What can we conclude regarding our mode of dress?

It is obvious what kinds of things God prefers in our mode of dress, but it is not so obvious which is a sin. Being well-dressed is not a sin in itself, it only becomes a problem when we use it to boast about ourselves, implying that we don't need God or to follow his ways. How does this match to what a true good God would want? A good God would not want us to harm others or endanger ourselves, yet he would also want us to enjoy the fruits of our good fortune. If we are great singers should we hide that away? If we can write profound poetry should we remain silent? If we are clever should we pretend to be stupid? If we are good-looking should we cover ourselves from view? If we rise to power should we never make a ruling? Which of these is the good and ethical thing to do? Can we not sing to please ourselves and others; write poems to charm and enthrall our audience; use our cleverness to advance what is good for the world; show our beauty to brighten others' days; and use our power to do what is best for all? What we should not do is use our singing to dismay, manipulate or offend; write poems to depress, frustrate or lead astray; use our cleverness to enslave, harm or deceive; show our beauty to conquer, snub or provoke to sin; or use our power to trick, cheat or dominate. These uses would be sins.

The true good God would want us to understand all these things and to turn from doing evil, which is harming others, to doing good, which is benefiting them. This tells us the true thinking we should use when each of us is choosing what we will wear.

* * *

In the Quran, God gave instructions for believers to not retreat in battle with disbelievers, unless swerving as a strategy for war or joining another company. [Quran 8:15-16] How should we interpret this?

The battles were for defending the faithful against attack by the armies of the disbelievers. These battles were supported by God, as advised to the believers by his Messenger, Muhammad. Allah had reinforced the believers with his heavenly angels. [Quran 8:9] It follows that retreating (literally: turning your back to the enemy) would be disbelieving and disrespecting God. This disrespect is similar to what we discussed under commandments one and two in the Hebrew Bible. As we said then, a good God may have found it easier to get his advanced ethical points across to ancient people by using simple, emotional terms that they would readily understand. Thus, he used the idea that he gets jealous when people worship false gods or idols in order to encourage good behavior in his believers. Those who retreated from a battle that God was supporting would not be acting in good faith, and so their actions would have to be condemned. We may be able to extend this idea further to say that we should show respect to all whom we find good. In any case, if we believe in God then we, rather obviously, should show respect towards him.

* * *

In the Quran, there is a verse that describes the killing of unbelievers. It says: "When the sacred months have passed, then kill the polytheists wherever you find them and seize them and besiege them and sit in wait for them at every place of ambush. But if they should repent and establish prayer and give zakah (alms-tax) then let them (go) on their way. Indeed, Allah is Oft-Forgiving and Most Merciful." [Quran 9:5] Some people have interpreted this to mean that

Muslims should kill all unbelievers, but this is a preposterous interpretation of the old document's instructions. What was God really driving at here?

The answer lies in the whole of the sura. This sura, 9, At-Tawbah (The Repentance), describes certain disbelievers (who were polytheists) who were given permission to travel to Mecca within a particular four-month period so that they could hear about Islam. Any who had violated their treaties with the Muslims and were found within the Muslim lands after the four-month period were to be executed, unless they repented or asked for protection from Muhammad. Those who sought protection were to be escorted to a place of safety, which was probably their homeland. The polytheists who broke their treaties with the Muslims were enemies, who had fought against Muslims and plotted to expel Muhammad from Mecca. Yet even they were to be spared if they repented, established prayer and gave alms-tax. The God who gave these instructions was inclined to peace, not violence, but also allowed his people to defend themselves from attack.

In spite of the reality of what is written in sura 9, some earlier (8th to 11th century CE) Muslim authorities interpreted verses 5 and 6 differently. One said that the meaning extends to all adult male disbelievers and that executing them was permissible if they had not been promised an Oath of Protection by a Muslim.

[Al-Shafi'i. *Kitab Al-Umm*, Maktaba Shamela, p. 1/293, (in Arabic):
https://shamela.ws/book/1655/278#p1]

Another said that verse 5 shows that Muslims should "Wage Jihad" against all non-believers. This was certainly an extreme view!

[Taymiyyah, Ibn. *Majmu Al-Fatawa*, Maktaba Shamela, p. 19/20, (in Arabic):
https://shamela.ws/book/7289/9537#p1]

Another said that polytheists should be converted by force, but Jews and Christians could be kept safe if they paid the poll tax in humility to the Muslims.

[Hazm, Ibn. *Al-Muhalla*, Maktaba Shamela, p. 5/362, (in Arabic):
https://shamela.ws/book/767/2058#p1]

Such interpretations do not match what a true good God would want. A true good God would want people to be helped, not harmed, wherever possible. That is the advanced ethical view. To interpret verses of old documents so that they support harming other people unnecessarily is sin.

Why would people interpret old documents sinfully? Unfortunately, there is nothing new here. This is our animal nature coming to the fore, driving us to support our own group at the expense of others. The people who play with meanings "accidentally on purpose" misinterpret what is written in order to deceive their followers into committing sins on behalf of their group. They put forward false arguments to get normal people to do what is usually only done by evil people, that is: harming as many people as needed in order to benefit yourself. This is not from God. It is evil masquerading as allegiance to God. It is sin.

* * *

So far we have been looking at what is in the old documents. Let's take a look at two more modern ideas now. These did not come directly from God, but they can help us understand more about what is sin.

The first more modern idea is from 1887: "Power tends to corrupt and absolute power corrupts absolutely." [Lord Acton, letter to Bishop Mandell Creighton, April 5, 1887] This is often stated simply as "Power corrupts."

This statement warns us of the dangers we face when someone is in power. The more power the person has, the more chance there is for the person to use it wrongly. The more power we allow someone to have, the more danger we face. The cause may be that power brings out the harmful side of people, or it may be that positions of power attract the more selfish types of people. The cause is not the important lesson, however. The important lesson for us is that we should expect this problem to occur, and we should, where possible, take steps to reduce its impact.

What is the meaning of this statement in terms of sin? For ourselves, we should be careful about taking on too much power as it may "corrupt" us. If we do have to take on some power, we should be very careful to remain "saintly" in our use of that power. We should remain ethical or good no matter what position we are in. We may even feel forced to reject an increase in our power if we are worried about our ability to resist its temptations.

The statement has political meanings for our society, obviously. It implies that there should be checks and balances on those who have any form of power, suggesting that a robust democracy is preferable to other forms of leadership. But in terms of sin, it tells us that a good God would not want us to risk corrupting ourselves by taking on more power than we could handle. Also, if we do have power we should use it only to benefit and not to harm others, as much as that is possible.

Even if a person has high religious authority, or a similar "high ethical authority", they should be monitored and controlled so that they stay on the path of doing good. We human beings have our animal weaknesses. We have to design our social structures with that in mind, just as we should design our own lives so that they help us to stay with what is good and avoid straying into what is sin.

* * *

The second more modern idea is: "You may fool all the people some of the time; you can even fool some of the people all the time; but you can't fool all of the people all the time." [attributed to Abraham Lincoln] Sometimes this is written as: "You can fool some of the people all of the time, and all of the people some of the time, but you can't fool all of the people all of the time." What can this tell us about sin?

Obviously, this saying promotes the virtues of democracy, but in terms of sin, it warns us that some people will try to fool others in order to benefit themselves and those close to them. These deceptive people may even harm others while they are in power. In fact, all kinds of people may try to fool others in order to benefit themselves and those they care for, it's not just in politics that this happens. It can happen in business, advertising, by influencers, writers, journalists... even some academics may try to fool others for their own benefit. Some people like to fool others for no other purpose than to cause harm to them, such as "trolls" on the internet. For such people, the "benefit" of seeing others upset is enough of a reward for their efforts.

We know that intending to unfairly harm others is sin, so we should aim to protect ourselves and "sinners" from causing such harm. Consequently, we should design our political systems to prevent, or at least reduce, the occurrence of harm achieved via deception. A robust democracy with a free press and the separation of powers is a known way to start. Allowing a dictatorship or other forms of forced leadership to exist is not the right way to go! Since people who like to fool us can operate in other areas than the government, we also need to implement systems that reduce their impact in those areas. This includes in business, advertising, the internet, news media, and even academic circles. The systems should reduce the potential damaging power of the deceptive people, while still allowing as much freedom as possible for everyone. Examples of such systems include having official bodies that monitor businesses and advertisers for deceptive practices; codes of conduct for journalists, academics, lawyers, organizations, and the like; internet monitoring requirements for internet service providers; and so on. We have such systems in some countries today. We need to continue with this work so that the world becomes a safer place for everyone.

There is a danger when we are trying to limit the ability of deceptive people to cause harm in that we may accidentally overdo it. We can, despite our good intentions, end up causing harm ourselves. We always have to keep in mind the principle that power can "corrupt us" when we are using it… even in those cases where we meant to use it to do good! Sometimes we should err on the side of reducing the strength of our safety measures in society, rather than overdoing them and impacting the innocent. We cannot do nothing, for that would be enabling harm to occur, but we also must not do too much. It is difficult to achieve, but there is no other reasonable solution available in our human world.

While we are implementing and running our human social measures, those who believe in God can be sure that he is, at the very least, observing and noting the actions of the deceivers as they do their dirty work within the world.

3. CONCLUSION

What are the consequences of sin? Sin has consequences that affect the individual, that is, ourselves, and it has consequences that affect other people, from those nearest to us and eventually all the way out to the whole world. What are these?

If we, as individuals, continue to harm ourselves, such as by smoking, overeating, under-exercising, and so on, then we will suffer physically. At some point our bodies will fail us, just as we have mentally and spiritually failed them.

If all of us, the people of the world, continue to sin, then we will all suffer. We will have poverty, unfairness, conflict, environmental destruction, and so on. Our world will continue to fail us, just as we have mentally and spiritually failed each other.

Sin leads to unhappiness, destruction and death. It may offer short-term benefits, such as money, pleasure and power for some individuals, but this will be at the expense of others. The "expense" may impact the people of today and it may even impact the people of the future, such as the environmental damage done by reckless businesses. It can affect only a few or it can affect whole nations and generations to come. All this so that a handful can be temporarily better off today!

The opposite of sin is to consider the consequences of what we want to do before we do it. Do we really want to cause harm to others... or even to ourselves? Do we want to go against what is good and right? Do we want to sin? Of course not!

Other people deserve our support, just as much as we deserve theirs... sometimes, they deserve it even more! We should "love our neighbor as ourselves."

God, (or, for some, the idea of God), has told us what is the right thing to do. He has given us a true view of what is sin and what is not. It is sin to seek to harm others, and it is not sin to seek to benefit them. The consequences of knowing that, of listening to God, are that the world will become a better place. The opposite leads to unhappiness, destruction and death. Understanding sin leads to life, for us all. A good God would want it that way.

AFTERWORD

I wrote this little book to help people. I do not want to profit from it. Accordingly, I am providing the ebook version for free, for people to use and distribute however they wish. The charge for the paperback version is to cover the printing costs only: I earn no royalties from these. People can also copy, print and distribute these however they wish. (See the copyright details at the start of the book for the Creative Commons license.)

I humbly apologize for any errors, oversights or annoyances. Regrettably, I have a poor human intellect and limited knowledge.

If you have any questions or comments that you would like to send me, please email me at: whatissin@outlook.com. I will do my best to reply.

Take care,

Geoff Pridham 2025

www.ingramcontent.com/pod-product-compliance
Lightning Source LLC
Chambersburg PA
CBHW011151290426
44109CB00025B/2568